GO FISHING FOR

TENCH

GO FISHING FOR
TENCH

GRAEME PULLEN

The Oxford Illustrated Press

The Oxford Illustrated Press

© 1989, Graeme Pullen

Reprinted 1989, 1991.

ISBN 0 946609 71 3

Published by:
The Oxford Illustrated Press Limited, Haynes Publishing Group,
Sparkford, Nr Yeovil, Somerset BA22 7JJ, England.

Haynes Publications Inc., 861 Lawrence Drive, Newbury Park, California
91320, USA.

Printed in England by:
J.H. Haynes & Co Limited, Sparkford, Nr Yeovil, Somerset.

British Library Cataloguing in Publication Data
Pullen, Graeme
    Go fishing for tench.
    1. Tench. Angling – Manuals
    I. Title
    799.1'752
    ISBN 0-94660-971-3

Library of Congress Catalog Card Number
    89–80217

Contents

Dedication

To the early tench writers who
painted the first picture.

Introduction

The idea of this series of 'Go Fishing' books, was to give youngsters, beginners and experienced alike, a few tips on catching a particular species of fish. Whether from sea or freshwater, every fish needs a specialised approach if any sort of regularity of capture is the angler's goal. Such knowledge can be gained from reading books, magazines and newspapers on fishing, but there is no substitute for hard-earned experience.

While all the technicalities may have been observed, there is always going to be that day when everything has failed; the rod has not bent, the float has remained motionless, and the keepnet lies dry. Many would believe it to be 'just one of those days', but the angler who has honed his perceptions after years of catching a particular fish will tell you otherwise. Experience leads to the sharpening of awareness and honing of instincts, and these same instincts are what makes the difference between a very good, productive fisherman, and one who observes all the technicalities, but fails to always catch.

Each species has little foibles and fancies, and I have tried to put in a few mentions of the methods that have been successful for me to outwit them. Doubtless other anglers will have other tricks up their sleeves to tickle the fish into feeding mood, but I can only speak of my own, and in this small book, can only pass on what I can to help you have the confidence to catch fish on every single session you fish.

The tench is one of our most beautiful fish; it is an olive green, gold-bellied fish with a tiny pig-like red eye. On the male fish in early season the pectoral and ventral fins stand out like scoops, and are used to good effect in driving them into a lily bed with your hook length! You cannot underestimate the power of a tench on medium-weight tackle. On a carp outfit you can stop them stone dead, but then if you want a good scrap, what could be better than an 11-foot float or leger rod with just a 1-lb test curve. Enough to land most tench, and enough to make you gasp at the bend it can take on when you hit a five pounder! Like many anglers, the tench was probably the first 'real' fighting fish I took from a lake as a youngster. First perch, then roach, maybe a rudd or two, then whoops! What's all this line doing leaving the reel? They may only have been $1^{1}/2$–2 lb fish then, but I well remember those evening sessions at a small pond at Fleet where the inlet ran off. (There's a car park with a screaming disco there now.) But then, oh yes, then you could see the float bobble and quiver as a cloud of pin bubbles came up around it. You knew, just knew as sure as the sun would rise, that the float would rise, then slide away. Sometimes the tench made the lilies and you strained before rod, line, or hookhold gave. To us youngsters they were monsters, to be laid out on the grass and watched as they flip-flopped around. You touched the sides, then just as quickly rubbed the slime straight onto your trousers or jumper. Well, we were kids, and didn't know what two-day-old tench slime on a sunny day would do for the bluebottle population! Since that early indoctrination into the mystery of the tench's summertime world, I have loved them. You never get an 'easy' tench. They all scrap to the net. In this book you may learn a few tips to put some more of them in your net. But never lose that respect for them. I think it was Fred Taylor who once wrote about childhood fishing haunts. 'Never go back' he said. There was never a more true word written, especially for the dyed-in-the-wool tench fisherman!

Tench

The pursuit of tench can be one of the most relaxing and rewarding pastimes. They are a species that would look pretty sluggish and quiet when viewed through the glass of an aquarium, but whack a hook in, and you are attached to one of the toughest fighters in stillwater. When I was knee high to a grasshopper the tench was always referred to as the 'Doctor fish'. Its slime was alleged to have healing properties, to such an extent that the other species would brush up against their slimy flanks and be cured of all ills. It was something written about for decades, and although I now think it's a load of old twaddle, I well remember Peter, a fellow schoolchum who suffered badly from acne. The tender age of thirteen is not a good time for meeting schoolgirls, and a bad attack of acne could just be the thing to wipe out your chances. Boiling hot flannel poultices issued by his mum, and tins of ointment had done nothing to improve his acne. So one day he decided to call on the 'Doctor fish' to help his ailments. Can you imagine the reaction next day when Pete arrived, his face smothered in tench slime that had dried like globules of glue, and smelt like nothing on earth! I don't think he's ever got married to this day!

The other fallacy was that because of the tench's powerful ju-ju qualities, the pike wouldn't eat them. Even now I never fish tench for pike, but I know they take them because I've had them nailed on the

Go Fishing for Tench

Close up of the business end. That mouth can take quite a big bait, so have no fear of using big bunches of lobworms, boilies or a large piece of bread flake.

way in, especially in pike-prolific Ireland, where Paul Harris once had a pike trying to eat a 3-lb tench he was playing! He later caught the pike on a dead perch, and it topped out at over 17 lb! Such are some of the myths surrounding this fish.

The British records for most species are usually taken by spawn-bound females, heavily pregnant with roe. The tench falls into this category, and many records are held with early season fish, when spawning is at its height. Back in 1963 the British rod-caught record for tench stood at 9 lb 1 oz, for a fish taken at Hemingford Grey. At that time a specimen tench would have been put at 5 lb, and a 6-lb fish would have been at the top of the range. Now improved techniques, new baits, and access to gravel pits and reservoirs has seen the record go several times, and the seemingly unassailable 9-lb Hemingford fish has been pushed to 12^1/$_2$ lb! The 5-lb specimen is now nothing to write home about, and has probably been pushed to 6 lb, with 7 and even 8-lb fish being the ultimate target aimed at by the big fish men. However, in Kiev there was reputed to have been a 16^1/$_2$-lb fish weighed, and I think the only thing restricting further British fish making 15 lb or so is temperature. If we had a better climate, more like that of southern Europe, I am sure the record would get up that far. However, only one person can hold the British record at any one time, so why bother with sleepless nights over whether you can break the record or not? There is plenty of fight in a 3-lb fish, and many pleasure anglers still regard 5 lb as a specimen tench. The reason many of the tench records get broken early in the season is because temperature dictates that is the warmest period for spawning.

Tench is one species that can tolerate very low oxygen in water, and the fish are therefore able to survive in almost stagnant ponds and stillwaters. This allows them to be retained out of water longer than any other fish, and I remember accounts of tench being kept alive in a wet hessian sack for up to two hours. This point is of no real use to the angler (as with any fish it's best to get them back in the water as soon as possible), but it does mean you can get good photographs because the fish can be kept out that little bit longer.

There is a golden tench, which is semi-albino, and used mostly for ornamental pond and lake work. However, I have heard several anglers over the years say they have caught 'golden' tench from ordinary stillwaters. Further investigation and photographs have seen one or two as probable releases, or escapees of the ordinary semi-albino ornamentals, but the others are in my mind just natural pigment variations of the standard olive-green variety. In dark, deep lily-choked waters you can get tench coming out very dark in colour, while in a milky clay-bottomed shallow lake they can come out totally light, making them seem an almost different species. It is merely the tench's way of adjusting to its habitat and surroundings, much like the chameleon changes its colour.

Depending on the temperature of our late spring/early summer period, the weight of the tench can alter from year to year, at the start of the fishing season on June 16th. If we get a very warm spring the tench are likely to start and perhaps finish spawning before the June 16th start. That means there is less likelihood of the British record being broken with a spawn-laden fish. Also the average weight of all female fish will be a little less. If we have a cool spring, with average temperatures below national average until the end of May, that same spawning may run on well into July, even to the end of that month. This means the weight average will be higher at the start of the season and the chances of the record being broken will be that much higher.

Seasonal fluctuations are not the only thing to affect fish size. Those living farther north in England will have slightly lower average temperatures, and I have heard of waters up there having spawning tench in early August. So if you really do want a record fish, look to a cool spring or travel north!

Tench will mainly spawn in shallow weedy water, congregating in shoals, and twisting and turning over each other in a generally excited manner. Most of the time they don't feed when they are in this phase, but they certainly feed with a vengeance when they have finished. They can lay over $3/4$ of a million eggs, which usually stick to the stems of underwater plants and weeds. From this number there is obviously a huge toll of casualties, but such a prolific egg lay helps maintain the stock of future fish. It was always said that you could never catch tiny tench, but I have found them myself when dragging swims really prolific with a growth of Canadian pond weed. On sorting through the weed on the bank I have found hordes of tiny two-inch tench fry. Every one was perfectly formed, and a light olive-green colour with that unmistakable small red eye. In some waters, the small tench disappear, presumably to the deeper water for safety, while other waters can be teeming with year-old catchable miniatures of the real thing.

Of course bait size is the limiting factor in so few small tench being caught. With twelve maggots on a size 10 hook, a bunch of lobworms or a half-inch boilie bait on the bottom, it is going to take them some

Tench

A secluded, wooded swim, an unrippled surface and the pin-like bubbles of a feeding tench. Sought after by anglers of all ages, the tench is undoubtedly a prime summer fish in Britain.

time to whittle the baits down to a size that will allow them to get it inside their mouth! For that reason it is no surprise to learn that the pole matchmen are the anglers who catch small tench consistently. They use very small hooks, tiny baits like squatts or bloodworm, and fish near the bottom using very sensitive float tackle. They are, after all, quite happy to catch small fish of any species.

Whether there appears to be a lack of mini-tench in any given water is no real cause for concern, it's the 2-lb-plus fish you will be after anyway. If you are catching those, there's a fair chance that with such prolific egg laying, some have survived to perpetuate the species. A strange phenomenon I have come across is this theory in reverse, where I have fished waters with lots of mini tench, and have had trouble finding any over 1 lb. You would think that the population of tench in the lake were naturally stunted, but when in the same water you have carp and other species growing on as usual, you start to wonder why you can't find the bigger tench. I have no answer to this myself. Perhaps disease hit all the adult fish, leaving only the following year's fry to go on? I don't know; it's a strange phenomenon and one which I hope someone will explain in the future.

Where to Fish Tench

Although the tench is a lover of slow-moving or static water, it is not uncommon to hit the odd fish in faster rivers. Certainly I doubt you would get a good net of fish from a fast river, more often than not it's just a single fish or two. Slow-moving rivers are more productive, but they have to be silt bottomed or muddy to hold any sort of numbers. The Thames has a few tench, but they are mostly confined to backwaters of eddies behind islands.

Canals are better still, having a barely perceptible flow, and occasionally having what is called a 'flash' where tench like to live. This is a larger circular area in the canal which was excavated during its construction to enable some of the load-carrying barges to turn around. The water in a flash may be a little deeper, and is certainly worth fishing for tench here—especially at the upcurrent end where the slight flow fills the flash. If you use a very slow sink cloudbait, it should drift away down current and bring up fish, even small fry. The attraction of the small fry darting around will draw the tench's attention and get them into the swim quicker than if you were fishing on the down current end of the flash. I use the term current only to give you some idea of where to fish. Some canals are of course almost static in high summer.

The best of the tench fishing comes from mud-bottomed old-established estate lakes, where the local fish stocks have balanced

Go Fishing for Tench

On a large lake or gravel pit you may have to reach a swim forty or fifty yards out with only loose feed. Use a weighted swimfeeder like this blockend, and ensure you cast accurately to the same place each time.

themselves out over the years. A tried and tested place to fish, your main problem may come in gaining access to fish there. There may be a silt build up over the decades which means there should be plenty of mud for the tench to root around in.

The other type of venue is the gravel pit. Many were dug to excavate gravel used in the construction of our motorways, and are therefore of fairly recent origin. Any new lake is rich in food, but a lake with a gravel bed is particularly so, because it will have clean water. Clean water will allow sunlight through, and this means weed growth will be fast. That in turn means the insect life will flourish, and any species, especially the tench, will pack on weight fast. They can grow to a large size in just six or eight years, before topping out at their best weight, and then dropping back in a natural cycle. Gravel pits probably offer the best chance of taking a large tench in excess of 5 lb.

Not to be forgotten are the reservoirs. We have some vast bodies of inland water, and they offer an almost unlimited potential. I say potential, for many are top trout fishing reservoirs, and access is restricted to only fly fishermen. A few are available to coarse fishermen, and it is from one of these that the present British record has come. In these large waters, depth is the restricting factor on weed growth, and so the tench become migratory, moving anywhere around the water in their search for food. Heavy and accurate baiting is essential if you want to locate them. Once an angler makes a good catch he either fishes there again pretty quickly, or tells his friends where to fish. News travels fast on the angling grapevine and shortly several anglers will be fishing that spot.

Previously the tench were moving about a large body of featureless water, feeding as they went. When there are several anglers, all throwing in bait in the same place, the tench become accustomed to that spot as an area of easy feeding, and may stay there for some time, even attract other passing tench by their feeding activity. The same situation occurs when you prebait, except you should have some sort of additional feature that you use to select a swim.

If you cannot find a feature, then you may spot clouds of pin-like bubbles floating on the surface. Once seen, and with a tench hooked when the bubbles are mushrooming around your float, they are never forgotten. Nor are they confused with carp bubbles which are larger, or the gas bubbles that pop up from the bottom as they are released, or a spiral of air bubbles that rise near some weeds and pop on the surface. Tench bubbles are almost foamy, and rarely pop for minutes on end; they just drift away with the air flow. The bubbles are generally caused by the tench's ability to drive its nose up to three inches in soft mud to disturb the bloodworm, or midge larvae. These are the main source of food for many species in a soft mud-bottomed lake, and tench suck them in with a mouthful of mud, swallow the bloodworm then blow out the mud particles through their gills. I believe they also do this when feeding on grains of groundbait, often ignoring a hookbait in the process. Not all 'blowing' or bubbling tench will take a bait, but it is at least an indication that they are present in the swim and feeding.

Techniques

Although tench are restricted to being most prolific in stillwaters, they respond well to a wide variety of baits and techniques. Some are quite specialised. As a general rule, the fishing gets harder after the start of the season, many anglers believing this is due to the excessive pressure they come under with a high influx of fishing activity. I have found this not to be the case. If you are fortunate enough to gain access to a little-fished water, even then you will find the fish starting to go off the feed as early as mid July. That leaves a scant four weeks when you can expect the best fishing, and if you cannot get the time off work to cash in on the easy fishing, you may find yourself struggling to scratch out a few fish in August.

When I say they go off the feed, this is something of a misnomer. Obviously the fish feeds; it has to if it is to survive. But I wonder if it is all tied up with natural feeding on insects? A few tench specialists I talked to said they thought the drop off in sport was due to water temperature. Having taken some temperatures over the years, both in freshwater and sea, you may be surprised to learn that it takes longer to cool down than you imagine. The only thing I can think of is that come the start of the season, and towards the end of June if the spring has been cold, the tench will just be getting over spawning. They will be ravenously hungry, which comes just at the time the anglers are out on the banks and putting in a lot of feed. Easy food for the tench to find, and easy fishing for the tench angler. However, even a little-fished water will produce well in those first four weeks, and that's without the additional food in the shape of anglers' baits. Which leaves me to draw the conclusion that the insect life may be at its greatest in the lake in mid July, when temperatures are at their highest, and the pupae have the highest hatch and activity rate. I can only theorise of course, but experienced tench anglers will tell you how the fish will continue to bubble out in front of you, yet ignore all hookbaits, which they must obviously be swimming near. I think they have got their noses down in the soft mud or silt, and are busy scooping up the bloodworm on the bottom.

This coincides with the problems that trout fishermen get at this time of year. It's called the Fly Fisherman's Curse, and occurs when the *Caenis* are hatching on the surface at such a rate, the trout become totally preoccupied with them. These are such tiny insects that the trout angler cannot effectively tie a small enough imitation, and even if he did, it would be like a needle in a haystack, as there are millions of these tiny insects in the water. All these *Caenis* start at the bottom of the lake bed, so I see no reason why the tench don't cash in on the prolific insect feed, ignoring the anglers' baits. I do however accept that some fish become wary, and bites get more finicky as the season wears on. But that doesn't explain why you can come across the same difficulties on a water that has rarely seen any previous angling activity.

While the tench do slow up through the middle of July and certainly into August, they gain a second 'wind' around early September. Again, many people think the fish are putting on fat for the coming winter, but as water temperatures don't drop considerably until about the end of October, there will be enough insect life about to keep them busy for several months.

A significant change worth noting, is that while the start of season, for the last two weeks of June, and around the first week of July, has a dusk and dawn requirement of fishing times, as the season goes on so the times change. By the end of July there may be nothing gained by either sitting out an entire night or setting up stall at 4 am, generally the time of day it gets light enough to floatfish. You may find the fish actually feed from 9 am onwards, and at times an angler

Techniques

The worst conditions for tench fishing. Midday, the sun blazing down from a clear sky and not a ripple on the water. I suggest you go home and return in the evening when the fish feed again.

will hit them from noon to 3 pm. On bright, still, sunny days when the sky is a piercing blue, I suggest a dawn start is still best, with the best of the fishing being over by the time 7 am arrives. Should you get one of those warm, muggy drizzly days with little or no wind, you can find the tench feeding into the midday hours and beyond. These particular conditions, especially during low pressure zones, are good for most species, but even on bright days I have had tench come to the float when I have started to doze off from boredom! One theory is that their feeding times are changing with the lowering angle of the sun, remember that in the rivers it is a noted fact that barbel actually migrate up a river at different times of the day as autumn sets in. Nobody seems to know why this should be so, and I can only pass on this information as an observation; it may just get you a few hours' sleep during the night in August and September. Perhaps the fish feed later because dawn is later? If you have a good feeding spell in early July at say two hours after dawn, it will be about 5.30 am. If in August you find the fish don't feed until 7.30 am it may be because dawn is that much later with the lowering of the sun and shortening of the days. That still doesn't explain why tench occasionally go dotty at midday, and again on some waters you may only get fish during the hours of darkness. All I can say is that as a *general* rule, all-night sessions are not so productive as those at dawn or dusk.

Assuming you want to fish right at dawn, I suggest you do two things. If you don't fancy a night session sleeping at the swim until dawn comes, it may still pay you to get to the swim the evening before and throw some groundbait in. This means when you turn up at first light all you throw in is your loose feed, which shouldn't disturb any tench just moving into the area from gaining confidence. If you turn up at dawn then disturb the surface with a heavy bombardment of groundbait, it may take an hour before fish move on to the feed. By then the sun will be up and you are cutting down on your time of productive feeding. By baiting the night before you can literally pick up a fish at half light on your first cast!

As for baits and methods the list for tench is almost endless. Although I have heard of the odd fish being landed on an 'exotic' bait like mackerel strip or eel tail, it must be regarded as a freak, for tench are true natural feeders and not scavengers or predators although

Paul Harris, angling advisor to the Irish Tourist Board, has seen plenty of big Irish tench hauls. Here he mixes in casters to his groundbait in order to make any browsing tench stay in the swim.

there may be a time during the early part of the season that they turn predatory; certainly when there is an abundance of newly hatched fry of other species about. I myself can't see fry used as bait being successful, and the tench must surely either disturb or eat the eggs of other species as it roots its way about the muddy bottom. I shall list only those baits which I consider to be constant producers of tench, together with a few which I regard as fringe baits, those which will take tench, but should be used only when the others fail.

There will also be a cross-section of other species likely to be caught on some of the baits, simply due to their size. When pre-baiting, or dragging a new swim you attract almost all the species present in that stillwater. Fry will probably be the first to move in. Attracted by the mushrooming clouds of mud, and disturbed organisms from the bottom, they feed more on insect larvae than the actual feed introduced. Following them will probably be the rudd, moving confidently into the swim, as the top layer of water is first to clear as the silt and suspended matter sinks, which is their natural depth of feeding anyway. They will take insects hatching that were disturbed from the bottom, plus any particles of groundbait that may be floating on the surface. Following them may be the roach and perch. The roach will often move onto maggots and casters first if they are the loose feed that was introduced, and the perch will be after the first hatchlings of fry that were attracted. Then you should get the tench and carp. All this fishy activity will undoubtedly attract the predator, and pike may lay off to the side of the swim waiting for his chance to nail a small roach or rudd that gets more involved with feeding, and drops its guard. By nightfall, and especially if you put in some worms, you get the eels, so therefore you can see even by fishing correctly for the tench you can still catch any one of a number of different species.

As for techniques of fishing I can only say you should ensure all hookbaits are firmly on the bottom. At certain times of the early season you may see an individual tench cruising in mid water. Only a couple of times have I heard of tench being taken on floating baits by carp anglers, and this was in water only a foot or so deep. Forget floaters in most circumstances. If you do spot an individual fish there is really only one way of catching him, as being daylight he won't be into a heavy feeding session. Do not pump in any groundbait or even catapults full of loose feed. That only spooks them. What you should do is rig up either a single size 8 hook and freeline, or floatfish with a tiny quill, a large piece of breadflake. Try to judge the direction the cruising fish is travelling, and cast way ahead of him, watching to ensure the flake sinks down and doesn't get caught on a piece of weed. It may rest visibly on the bottom in which case you get the added excitement of watching that tench actually take the bait.

I first did this in a boat on Fleet Pond near my home. I had been fishing a prebaited swim all night, and had picked up a few roach and a couple of tench. About 8 am I started poling around standing on the front and looking for signs of fish moving round the margins, with a view to baiting a different area. Using polarising glasses I spotted quite a few tench, not in groups, but drifting about singly, their green backs showing black in the two-foot-deep water. It was obvious why I had failed to 'bag-up' the previous night, as those fish were almost in a doze as they swam slowly along. I could get very close to them before they spooked, so I tried angling the boat to bring me up behind them, and standing on the bow I cast a floatfished flake well ahead of them. If I got it right I would see the tench stop, then move forward carefully as it inspected the flake, and if it passed the test, suck it in. The first few I missed through striking too early, but then I waited until the float slid away, and took a fish every time. I only had a few, but it just showed by observing and adapting, I had caught more in bright daylight, than I had all night cramped up in the boat!

I would suggest that it is very rare to take them on the drop with a moving bait. The only time I have known this happen was when match fishermen were feeding a swim with a constant supply of loose feed and not much groundbait. Small loose feed like maggots are taken by the other species are well, which means the tench have to come up off the bottom if they are to get in on any of the feed. I see no point in adopting this little-and-often technique for tench, as you lose too much feed to the other species. You need to get everything down on the bottom where the tench are feeding naturally on bloodworm and the like. The two basic methods of catching them are by floatfishing or legering.

Go Fishing for Tench

Floatfishing

Many people think floatfishing is a method devised to suspend a bait at a predetermined depth, much like shark fishing. Occasionally this may be so, but for tench it is an early warning bite indication, and is far more efficient than most people realise. When legering you invariably use some form of bobbin for the tench to pull unhindered. This will move up towards the butt ring several inches before you strike. To eliminate this unwanted length of line, you can make your bite indicator point nearer the fish, namely from the rod top itself. Now you can use either a swingtip which just takes the tension up on the line from the rod top, or the quivertip. The latter is a screw-in indicator that is really a very thin extension of the rod top. Ideal for letting you see those twitchy bites. If you want an even better bite indicator you must place the indicator as close to the hookbait as possible. Therefore a float does the job better than any of the aforementioned. You can shot it down so just an eighth of an inch is showing, which makes it far more delicate than anything else. That is the ideal. Of course it can only be used under certain conditions, and being sensitive it is susceptible to a variety of different conditions.

On shallow lakes with a round circumference, you get an undertow. This will continually drag the float under. The wind can push it along and out of position from the baited area. The intended area of fishing may not be close enough to reach with the type of float you are using. To choose the best type of float is always difficult. Like so many other fishermen I have far more floats than I ever use, and only a few are ever used for fishing. Years ago a porcupine quill or a swan quill was the best to use. It was long, slender, and the top could be shotted down to the required showing. Those were attached by passing the line through a wire eye at the bottom of the float, which was then held in position by a rubber sleeve or ring at the top.

They caught plenty of fish, but over the years, constant demand for improved match fishing techniques saw a boom in the waggler float, which came either as a straight stem waggler, or a bodied variety. These floats were attached to the line through the bottom ring only, in order to facilitate sunk lines. The only real way to beat the wind is to make sure the line between the float and rod top is below the

Techniques

Clear a hole in the lilies to bait up into. The few lilies in the foreground of this picture should be removed to avoid snagging up any hooked tench.

Go Fishing for Tench

surface where the ripples and breeze can't work to push it out of place. To sink the line, you must first cast further than the baited area, then wind fast several times with the reel handle to pull the line beneath the surface film. You may have to stop once or twice and let the float pop up so you know where it is in relation to the swim.

You can set the float so the bait is just resting on the bottom, but this is only ideal when the air is still and no wind acts on it. You get first class bite indication, but remember when I said earlier about the fish throwing up clouds of foamy pin-like bubbles as they feed? What can happen is the tench bump into the line causing the float to dip. You either strike and miss the fish completely, or you 'wing' it and find it foul-hooked, which of course is not the intention. More likely you will strike and spook the fish, which may bolt, taking any others that were feeding, along with him!

I prefer to fish with the float set about six inches overdepth. To do this you simply plumb the swim setting the float at the required depth, then slide it up an extra six inches. I put a number 8 shot at six inches from the hook just so it trails on the bottom and slows or stops any slight drift movement of the float. When a fish bumps the line the float will jar to one side rather than pull under. The type of bite you get with this rig up is a trembling of the float, which then angles away before sliding under. If you set the float more than six inches overdepth, say a foot or so, the float will ride along the surface rather than slide under.

Remember that the float is an indication device and you don't have to strike only when it disappears below the surface. If it is gliding along flat then strike! The fish has picked up the bait and is rising in the water, as well as swimming along. He may well swallow it, but he also has the option of spitting it out if you leave him too long. Also if it starts moving against the wind or ripples you must strike. If it drags off towards the lilies you can bet the fish is just starting to feel the float and is wondering whether to bolt into the tangle and sanctuary of lily stems. Hit him before he has a chance to make up his mind.

The other method of rigging up a float is the lift method. This was devised many years ago, I would imagine to get a really positive bite. You set the float up the same as before, with about ten or twelve inches of hooklength lying on the bottom. In the place of the single

An angler applies the pressure to a tench on the Basingstoke Canal. In narrow stretches of water like this one, play the fish out quickly in order to leave other feeding tench undisturbed.

number 8 shot that avoids dragging with the wind, you put the bulk of your shot. This anchors it firmly to the bottom, and stops it dragging out of position, even with a strong wind. You need not shot the float down so low as a quarter or half an inch. You can leave it sticking up an inch or two inches. This aids visual detection, and is handy in times of failing light conditions. The tench comes along, picks up the bait, and as he rises a little off the bottom he takes up the balance of those shot on the bottom. From the angler's viewpoint he will see the float dither, then rise and fall flat. It will stay flat for as long as the tench supports those shot, but when he moves off, the float will slide beneath the surface.

There are two schools of thought as to when you can strike. Older anglers feel it best to resist the impulse to set that hook until after it has sunk out of sight. Other tench anglers, myself included, feel that you should strike the instant the float rises and falls flat. The tench after all is supporting those shot, and feeling any undue resistance has every opportunity to spit that bait out. This is particularly noticeable towards the end of July onwards into August, when the fish have been caught a few times, and are getting a bit cagey. For that reason alone I would suggest using the 'lift' method only at the start of the season, when you are fishing larger baits like boilies, bread flake or worms, and want to ensure you know it is a tench messing with the bait, and not some 3-oz perch! It is also a useful method on breezy days, when your swim is still close enough to floatfish, but shotting the waggler down to a pip makes it continually give false bites.

If you start fishing at dawn the light level will be low and a yellow top float stands out best. You may find as the sun rises that a patch of reflective glare is right where your baited area is. If possible leave your float out in the chosen position, then move round to one side of the swim or the other, and line up the float's position with something behind it, maybe a landmark on the opposite bank, a branch or shadow line. Get an idea where you would cast to from this new position, then move your tackle round, and recast so you can see the float better. Remember if you use waterline shadows as bearings for casting to, that the sun swings round in a high arc during mid summer. Therefore those shadows will move sometimes, so I would suggest using a fixed bearing like a bush, tree or other swim on the opposite bank. If you have a small tight swim and cannot move to one side or the other, try using a black top float. These stand out really well against a white glaring surface, and should you want to cast to the side into a patch of shadow, simply paint the top of the float white using a bottle of Tippex. This is a trick used by match anglers, and the white tippex can be removed with pressure from your thumbnail if you want to change back to a black float tip.

Floatfishing is possibly the most enthralling way of landing tench, specially when fishing amongst lilies or rush stems, which not only add to the setting, but give you a better reference for bearings to see if the float has been moving. The advantage of early warning bite indication is a bonus to the tench angler, and while it is a pleasurable way of catching them, I feel it may not be the most successful.

Legering

When you leger a bait on the bottom, you are certain that it is in the feeding region of the tench. You can fish a bait in conjunction with a swimfeeder, or a plain bomb weight. You can use running legers, fixed paternosters or bolt rigs, much like those used by the carp fishing fraternity. Indeed I would say it is the carp angler who has been responsible for most of the new techniques now being used to good effect by the tench angler. They caught a lot of very big tench when baiting swims up for carp, and if you remember, I mentioned before that baiting a swim pulled in a wide variety of species.

Although a by-product of carp methods, new baits and rigs were quickly adapted by the modern tench angler. Gone were the traditional methods of 'lift' bite floats, crowquills and a lobworm, although these still catch fish. In came leger rigs and hair rigs, bolt rigs and balanced paternosters.

When floatfishing or legering one of the primary requirements is for accuracy of hookbait placement. Previously I have mentioned using the lilies and other floating weeds as your casting guide, but on a featureless large water, or where you have to cast any great distance to reach a feature, you need some sort of swim marker. Providing the club by-laws permit it, I see no reason for not going out either with a pair of chest waders, or a boat, and putting in a permanent swim

Go Fishing for Tench

While floatfishing for tench is popular, legering on the bottom generally produces bigger fish. This angler fishes with a pair of Optonic sounders and bobbin indicators on an Irish Tench lake.

marker. This can be adapted from a bamboo cane, perhaps with a couple of dabs of white paint on the tip that clears the surface. This can be rammed, thick end down, into the mud and should stay there for some time. By using a bamboo pole, should you hook a big tench he may take your line round the back of it. Anything too strong will act as a snag for the fish to break the line. With a soft willowy bamboo cane, providing you sandpaper down the rough notches first, the line will pull right over the top, as it bends either way. The bamboo cane is fine as a daytime marker, or even silhouetted in the water reflection on a moonlight night.

But on windy, cloudy or moonless nights you are going to experience some difficulty in outlining it. A good way to overcome this is simple and extremely effective. A large majority of tench waters can be quite shallow, around three to five feet deep. Using either the chest waders or a boat go out to your swim and drop a

The author adjusts his bobbin indicator as the sun appears through early morning mists over Frensham Great Pond, the scene of many big tench catches. This is a prime time for

Above: An angler battles it out with a fish hooked from a proper fishing stage. If you have the facilities and permission, make any sort of platform to keep yourself above boggy ground close to an area known for tench movements.

Facing page: Slow moving waters like canals offer good sport but rarely produce tremendous bags. In these conditions, tench respond best to light feeding of cloudbaits and loose feed.

Left: The gravel pit provides some of the best fishing for big tench which grow quickly in the food-rich waters. The careful location of gravel bars and depth changes will help the angler to place his baited patch near the routes of patrolling tench.

Above: This is an ideal swim for tench. A good colour in the water, a bed of lilies and some thick weed offering food. Fish in the clear water to the edge of the lilies, loose feeding with a little groundbait.

Left: Water lily in flower. These plants offer the tench shade during the sunny hours so fish close to them with either float or leger. If you need to clear a swim, make sure you only make a hole large enough to hold the bait rather than ripping up all the lilies.

Facing page: Water lilies grow best in shallow water up to five feet deep so why not move some to favoured areas and create a holding area for the following season?

Above: A rare shot of a miniature tench. These do not show up regularly and remain in many waters at this size before being caught by anglers when they reach 1 lb or more in weight.

Facing page: Back goes another fine fish. If you don't want a catch picture, it is preferable to put the fish back straight away. This doesn't deter other fish from entering the swim as anglers believed years ago.

Left: Small baits like maggots, casters and hemp come into their own later in the season when the fishing gets harder. They account for some good August bags of fish.

Nigel Newport looks pleased with this fine haul of tench taken on a cocktail of sweetcorn tipped with worm. The swim was dragged and baited the previous evening.

marker made from a length of one-inch diameter plastic piping. It's easily obtainable from a plumber's wholesaler. Buy a piece about seven feet long, and blank off one end by filling it with about 1 lb of lead. Make sure you don't pour the molten lead into the pipe otherwise it melts straight through. Better to make a pre-shaped mould from some baking foil, pour the lead into that and let it set. When cool, you simply slot it inside the pipe and araldite into place. The other end can be blanked off with a plug of dowel. Then you paint the top two feet with white gloss paint, and you have your marker. Simply drop it into position and retrieve it after you've finished your session.

As a feasible 'night-sight' I would advise gluing into the top end a thin clear plastic tube, maybe an old pen casing. Into this you can slot one of those Cyalume chemical lightsticks that should provide light for an entire night session. These lightsticks are made by a company called American Cyanamid, and consist of a plastic tube full of liquid, inside which is another phial of liquid. To activate it into light, you simply bend the whole tube until a crunching sound indicates you have broken the internal phial. On mixing, these two chemicals provide light.

These lightsticks really are very handy, as the small versions are ideal for using as bobbin indicators, while the larger models, up to six inches in length, can be used as swim markers. They also come in a variety of chemical light colours: green, yellow, red, blue and white. Of these, the best for the job is undoubtedly the green, and the softest is the red. The light from these larger nightsticks is considerable and can be seen way across the lake, up to four hundred yards away. Make sure you use the right models, as they now come in different light intensities and durations. You can get a high intensity yellow for instance, that provides enough light to read a book, but lasts only thirty minutes. The type most suitable for swim markers and bobbin indicators would be the twelve-hour green, which still gives out a lot of light. Another tip that is worth knowing concerns the temperature. On a hot summer night the chemicals glow brighter, but for a shorter period. The reverse is true on cold nights. At the start of the season you will only be getting a few hours of darkness, perhaps six hours from 10 pm to 4 am, right through to mid July. Being a liquid, the

Cyalume lightstick can be taken home and frozen solid, which allows you to have an 'instant' light the moment you thaw it out! If you buy a twelve-hour lightstick and take along a thermos flask of ice, you can pop it in the flask at 4 am when it gets light, then freeze it solid when you get home. This would be more applicable to the smaller Cyalumes than the larger one for swim marking, as you will obviously not wish to disturb that one until you finish the session.

The other more common method of placing a retrievable swim marker is this. Find a piece of polystyrene about ten inches long. It will probably be white anyway, but if not, repaint it white. Cut it so the shape resembles a cylinder. Tie some 30-lb nylon to the centre of the cylinder and wind round about two feet more than the depth you intend fishing. You can even do this at the bankside of a new swim, providing you plumb the depth first. When you have wound all the line around the spool, tie on a few old bolts, or a non-lead weight of about three ounces. Then you just throw it out to your swim, and the weight sinking through the water unrolls the line from around the cylinder. The weight sinks to the bottom and acts as an anchor. By making the line about two feet longer than the depth it means the polystyrene will drift away until it reaches the end, thus leaving the line from the weight to the polystyrene cylinder at an angle, not vertical.

To retrieve this, all you do is cast another weight with a large barbless carp hook or barbless treble to one side or other of the marker, where on retrieving you snag the anchor line. Yes, it's re-usable! If you are really pushing your baits out some distance, you will have to make your polystyrene cylinder a lot smaller, so that it fits across your catapult. Remember that however far you catapult it out, you have to cast that same distance in order to retrieve it.

A final tip on swim markers. Never put the marker down right in the centre of your swim, or in a direct casting line behind it. Place it to one side, and parallel to the baited area, and you will minimise the number of fish that swim over it. If they do of course there is no problem anyway, as the marker will be towed back in with the fish. Simply unravel it, then place it back where you want it. Accuracy of hookbait in your baited area is something that you must take the time to master. There is little doubt that not only can it give you more fish, but with the preoccupation of feeding, those tench are going to give you a much more confident bite.

Moving on from the use of Cyalume lights for bobbin indicators, I feel mention should be made of the different types of bobbins you can use. Having already heard of the float, quivertip and swingtip, all the bobbin does is to register the bite from a length of slack line between the first butt ring and the second ring. All this bobbin should do is to take up the tension on the line, making it as straight as possible to the hookbait, but without causing any undue resistance to a taking fish. The lightest bobbins are best in flat calm conditions, used without the sliding spike that many anglers use to prevent them blowing about in windy conditions. You want that tench to feel as little resistance as possible, while using a bobbin that gives you the earliest visual indication of a bite. I used to put a folded piece of silver paper on the line, and caught dozens of tench using this for years. You could put a kink in the silver paper so any ambient light from the moon would catch it and allow you to see its every movement. This saved me running a torch all night, or indeed any form of light to illuminate the bobbin.

You could also make various weights of bobbin, by putting extra folds into it. The best are made from cooking foil. However, the one drawback with this is that every time you strike the paper flies off into the grass or bushes. I tried making them into a circular shape, but occasionally they would ride up the line as a fish took, and create drag in the rod ring. It would only be slight, but at the time when the tench start to get a bit finicky, particularly around early August, I felt that minor resistance was sometimes responsible for a few dropped bites. In difficult sessions it was bad news to sit for several hours, get a single bite, then have it stopped because the fish felt the drag of the bobbin.

Then, a friend from Essex, Jerry Airey, came down to stay for a weekend. I noticed he was using circular plastic bobbins with a split in them, that were both light, and didn't stick to the line, even in wet weather. He explained that he simply adapted some of those plastic coils that are used as binding spines for various size notebooks and scrapbooks. By cutting off the paper first he was left with twenty or more coils of plastic which he then cut into individual rings. You can get various sizes of book spines and thereby alter the weight, plus you can get, as well as pure white, jet black ones too.

The latter are especially good for when the rods might be placed in rests over the surface of the water. You might have to wade out between some rushes for instance or you can get eye strain from staring at a white bobbin, against the sheen of light on the water. The black bobbin provides you with a harder silhouette. But when your swim is overshadowed by trees and bushes and it is cloudy or perhaps twilight, then a black bobbin is no good, so you simply change to a white one.

For additional weight, if you are fishing a lake that is shallow and has some undertow that continually drags the bobbin up to the butt ring, you simply pinch on a shot to the edge of the plastic. You rarely lose them either as they have to be opened before clipping on the line, so they don't fly off into the unknown on the strike! If it is too windy and the bobbins start crashing into each other you can slide them onto a spike and keep them rigid.

I must confess that although many tench anglers legering today use what is known as monkey-climb indicators, I still prefer a loose-hanging bobbin. My reason is again to avoid any drag factor incorporated by the bobbin sliding up the spike. I first started by using spikes made from straightened coat hanger wire. By placing them in the ground, and sloping them towards the rod ring, they worked quite well. But I wanted even less drag, so I changed to 18-SWG gauge stainless steel wire, obtainable from model shops, and used as undercarriage supports on the wheels of radio-controlled model aircraft. This is very thin and provides barely any drag at all. My other dislike of spike supports, although in very windy weather you simply must use them, is that of missed dropback bites. When you freeline a large bait for tench, a large piece of flake, a bunch of lobworms, or boilies, you have just the weight of that bait resting on the bottom for the bobbin to pull tension against. If you use something like the old washing up liquid top caps for a bobbin, you find it can be too heavy on the spike to register a gentle forward tug. On the other hand a light bobbin of the circular type described does not have enough weight on its own to register a drop-back bite when resting on a spike. A heavy bobbin on a freelined bait will continually

Techniques

Tench survive well out of water but you still need to get them back in the water as soon as possible after capture. Arrange a plastic sheet for the fish to lie on, and organise the cameras so everything is done quickly.

drag it back down to the ground, and thus pull the bait out of position. As late-season tench are noted for being finicky I feel it far better to have some sort of register of a drop-back bite using a light bobbin without resting it on the spike.

Admittedly this can be something of a pain in windy weather when they blow about, but the simple method to minimise this movement is to shield them from the wind. This can be done by positioning your brolly as a wind shield, or even making a small wind shield the height of the rods, so the wind is kept off the line held by the bobbins. These would only be minor points at the start of the season when the tench are bolder in feeding, but as far as I am concerned you want to get the best chance of a fish, regardless of time of year and conditions. Also, in a full gale the fish probably won't feed to any degree anyway, so there's no point in going out. Better to wait until conditions permit easier indications.

Other bite indicators that work for the tench are swingtips and quivertips. Both are attachments screwed into the tip ring of your rod, and being closer to the fish, and without the drag or friction factor of line drawn across the rod rings, they are probably the most sensitive indicators other than a float. I would venture the suggestion that both indicators are used in conjunction with the smaller range of hookbaits: sweetcorn, seed baits, maggots and caster. The reason for this is when you use a large mouthful of bait like a bunch of lobworms, large boilies or a bumper piece of flake, you need a foot or two of line to be taken up allowing the fish several bites at getting the larger hookbait inside its mouth.

The swingtip moves only the full length it hangs at, say five inches from vertical to horizontal; not enough for a medium sized tench to get a bait well inside its mouth. Of course you still get a perfect upward swing of the tip, and not unnaturally you strike. But you either miss that fish completely, or fight him for a period of time only to have the hook fall out because it was only holding the fringe of the mouth.

A similar situation occurs when you use a quivertip, perhaps with the tip moving only some three inches if it is soft. Thus large baits should be used with either float or bobbin as indicators, and the smaller hookbaits, where an early strike will often see the bait inside the mouth, is better. Of the two I much prefer the use of the quivertip. It's not that much more sensitive, but I just enjoy its use more. Casting seems to be easier too, as the swingtip can occasionally flop round on the cast and tangle the line. It also flops about when you 'feather' the edge of the spool in mid cast to slow the terminal tackle down if you look like over casting the swim.

Swingtips can be home made from a piece of fibreglass or thin cane, but you need to pick up the screw-in adaptor and set of tiny rings from your local tackle shop. To counteract any underwater tow or drift in a shallow water you can buy swingtips with various weights. Alternatively some anglers like to add their own weight, simply by winding a few turns of lead or soldering wire round the tip eye. After casting out, wind the line to sink it as previously described in float fishing. This usually means overcasting the swim, which has the added bonus of not frightening the fish if the swim is very shallow. Let the line settle for a few seconds, then take three or four turns of the reel handle after placing the rod in the rests. This straightens everything out on the bottom. The tip will most probably be out on the horizontal, so simply back wind the reel until it hangs almost vertical, just taking the strain on the line. With this swingtip method you immediately see any drop-back bites, especially if you set the tip at 45 degrees to the horizontal. It's best to sit with the tip parallel to the bank, so you can see the movements easier.

Swingtips were first popularised by bream fishermen many years ago, and are used today by match anglers and pleasure anglers alike, for a wide variety of species. Swingtips are of little use on a fast-flowing river where the pace of the current keeps pulling the tip out straight, although they can be used on slow flowing rivers and drains, which suits the tench a lot better anyway.

Quivertips are another screw-in attachment to the tip ring, or they can be fitted as a spliced-in part of the rod itself. This latter method is in my opinion far superior, although of course you are governed by what poundage that quivertip is rated at. The quivertip works with the line being tight from terminal tackle to rod top, and is so sensitive that even the tiniest bite is registered as a tweak or a tremble. With a screw-in tip you can buy various strengths of curve i.e. 1 oz test curve, $1^1/4$, $1^1/2$, 2, $2^1/2$ and even 3-oz to counteract the flow in fast rivers.

I use the quivertip in conjunction with small baits, something like a swimfeeder filled with groundbait and maggot mix, and maybe a couple of maggots on the hook, I use it from August onwards when the fish are starting to go off the feed a bit, and I need to strike at the tiniest bite. In still waters, you need to use the lightest curve possible, maybe 1 oz or $1^1/2$ oz. Occasionally you may need to step it up to overcome undertow, but the lighter you can use the better.

Simply overcast the swim and retrieve to sink the line, then place the rod in the rest. Again you need to fish with the rod top almost parallel with the bank to get the maximum vision on the tip's movement. Just after you have positioned the hookbait in the swim, leave the rod for a few seconds, then tighten or slacken the tip until the tiniest tension is applied to it. If you put too much tension in it, and curve it round, you don't see the bite. If you have it lying straight from the rod top with the line slack you can't see a slack line or drop-back bite. What you need is a happy medium, with just a small amount of tension in the tip.

Quivertips don't create so many problems on the cast, and I find them excellent when fishing at long range where accuracy of casting is required. The only problem that you may come across, and this also applies to fishing closer in with the swingtip, is that of line bites. Where the line from rod top to terminal tackle is kept taut, it means the line running through the water may be an inch or so above the lake bed, rather than lying on top of it as would happen when you used bobbin indicators. Any fish that blunder into this line are referred to as 'liners'. They make the tip react sharply, then relax equally as quickly as the line flicks clear of the fish. Only experience can help you in distinguishing 'liners' from proper bites. However, sometimes in the darkness or even half light of dawn you may not be casting and retrieving the tackle exactly over the baited patch. If the gear is out past the feed, then you get the self same liners, which should indicate to you that you need to come in closer to where the fish are rooting about. So in effect the liners can be deemed useful! Also if the undertow is severe on a lake, you can mount the quivertip, not the swingtip, high up off the horizontal, to keep as much line clear of the water drag as possible, even at 45 degrees to the horizontal.

On the other hand you may be fishing in blustery conditions, with a near gale howling straight into your swim, but there is no undertow. Then you need to do the reverse, and sink as much line as possible to keep it out of the wind, and maximise bite detection. Both these types of tips can be painted with Tippex typing correction fluid if you are positioned with the tip in a dark shaded area or bankside. Probably the most popular method is to paint either type of tip either red or white, or black and white in sections, like a zebra crossing, which allows for fishing both dark patches or through surface glare.

Matchmen also make use of what is known as a target board. This is usually a black painted board, about twelve inches square, that is screwed into a bank stick attachment. You position it behind either tip, and can see any small movements against a grade of lines marked

Techniques

The beautiful tench mixes well with other ornamental fish such as carp, goldfish or even this specimen Golden Orfe. Both these fish fell to maggots on a private Wiltshire water.

on the board. Personally I find watching the tip against one very difficult. I keep getting mixed up with which is on the board, and which is my tip, especially difficult in the half light of a night session.

From the use of these tips I feel it worth making note of an age-old method that nobody seems to use nowadays; the float-leger. If you recall I said earlier that the most sensitive bite indication comes from an indicator nearest the bait, in most cases the float. The float-leger is a combination of methods that allows a good distance to be fished, but still retains the sensitivity of the float. You rig up as normal with a running leger rig, but have a float fixed at the correct depth. You cock it simply by applying tension to the line with a turn or two of the reel handle and it is ideal for fishing anything up to four or five feet deep. Anything over that and you need to mount the rig as a sliding float. This means the float is free running on the mainline but is stopped at the required depth by a stop knot of nylon monofilament, tied in at the required depth. Always make sure the float, whether sliding or fixed, is set slightly overdepth. This way you can tighten up slowly on it to set it at the right amount showing above water. The major drawback with this method is surface drift which will often drag the float slowly beneath the surface.

The sliding float can of course be used on its own, for standard float fishing in very deep water. However, in my experience, very deep water means little sunlight penetration, which in turn means little or no weed growth. That all adds up to no tench, so try not to fish anything over about eight or ten feet.

The one main advantage of the float leger, and the sliding float is when gravel pit fishing. Many specialist tench fishermen make it their business to learn where the gravel bars and drop-offs are in order to locate the patrolling routes of the larger tench. Many of the big fish were thought to be solitary, but in my opinion there are just a lot fewer 8-lb-plus tench in any water, in relation to three pounders! Some of these gravel bars, which undoubtedly attract fish, are productive areas to put the feed. I think they are popular because as I've just mentioned, deep water equals fewer weeds, plus the shallower the water, the quicker it warms up, and the natural food requirements of the tench are in these areas.

Some gravel pits were excavated by the 'throwback' method. This means the spoil was heaped up in ridges behind the machine, and the pit bottom will therefore be undulating. When fishing a standard leger rig your line may run over the top of one or more of these gravel bars, and you can often get cut off on the strike, as the line runs over the stones. By casting out into a gully or onto another bank or ridge, using a slider the bulk of the line will be in the upper surface layers. When you strike your main line should be fairly clear of the bottom.

Legering used to be a fairly basic technique, you slid a weight up the line, stopped it with a shot, then tied on the hook at the required distance from the lead. The main drawback with this is line friction. Now the better method is to fish with the lead set away from the main line on what is known as a link. This allows a taking fish more freedom of movement before coming into contact with any friction where the line passes through the lead. Instead of using a shot pinched onto the line, which weakens it enough to cause breakage, you can use a nylon tube and peg called a leger stop which doesn't harm the line. If you do need to make a change in the distance of this leger stop, don't slide it up the line under pressure. Pop out the peg, move the nylon sleeve, then put the peg back in. I can't tell you how many times I've slid that leger stop up and down the line, then hooked a tench and cursed when the line broke. I still do it occasionally when I'm in a rush, even though I may be creating a weak spot! Try not to follow in these footsteps and take a little more time.

The final method that can be used, although I rarely use it for tench myself, is that of the bolt-rig. A technique used by the carp fishermen, it consists of threading the bait, usually a boilie or paste bait onto a piece of 1-lb nylon line. The line is then tied about one inch onto the bend of the hook, so in fact the bait is clear of the hook, or the thicker mainline. This hook is stopped about six inches from the lead, and the lead itself is much heavier than you would normally require, up to $1^1/2$ or 2 oz. The fish comes along, sucks in the bait, without feeling the 1-lb nylon link. Confident that it's all OK it throws the bait farther into its mouth, but then feels the hook. Alarmed it bolts away, banging into the taut line held by the lead, the weight of which is enough to hold the hook in place, until the angler can strike. Most times, the angler fishes with the anti-reverse of the

Go Fishing for Tench

Always use a long landing net pole if fishing with light float tackle, and net the fish as soon as possible.

reel in the 'off' position, so the rod doesn't get dragged in! Obviously this is a self-hooking method, and while many feel it takes the skill out of fishing as an art, it is nevertheless highly successful.

The carp angler can scale this entire rig down to suit his bait requirement, and use only say, a 1-oz lead as the weight. This technique is best used on a water where carp and tench mix freely together, and where there are plenty of carp anglers putting feed in. Tench soon find these baits, and if they are small enough, will devour them avidly, much to the detriment of the carp fishermen. If you follow their pattern of baits, and use a scaled down bolt-rig technique, you can pick up good tench not only in the harder mid season period, but you have every chance of hitting into a decent carp or two as well!

There are other leger rigs and variations that are personal favourites to individual anglers, but for those interested in catching tench consistently rather than worrying about size, the aforementioned methods should give them a bit of activity. Tench can be incredibly finicky feeders, or they can engulf baits almost as soon as they hit the bottom. I can't explain why, and I doubt if there is any angler that can answer that one. Fishing is fishing, and if we knew all there was to know about a species there would be no interest in trying to catch them.

Baits

Just as with all the techniques described nothing is guaranteed, the same goes for the culinary requirements of the fish. They will at times eat virtually anything, so a run through of baits available is worth looking at. This is not a list with any order of preference. Much of the time it is the angler who has preference rather than the fish. I grant you there are definitely times when a certain bait will outfish any other, but usually this is on a particular water, and only lasts for a limited period of time. The tench either become wary of that bait being used, or they simply go back on to natural feed, which is more prolific.

As an example, early in the season, the angler will have to wean the tench off their natural diet of bloodworms, and onto their favoured hookbait. Remember that the tench will have seen little of an angler's bait through the preceding winter, and certainly nothing for $2^1/2$ months of the close season. All they know is the natural food available. By July they will have become accustomed to finding angler's feed in the water, simply because the start of the season sees the most angling pressure on. Once you get to mid-July, the anglers start to thin out, and although those left may still be feeding quite heavily, they cannot feed every swim in the lake! The tench in one area find the angler's food particles, while those at the other find nothing and thus revert to natural food. The following are examples of successful baits, that I can only suggest you use at varying times of the year. They certainly work, but I cannot tell you exactly when they will work!

The good old standby of **breadflake** must surely be one of the most neglected baits. Yes, I realise many think it's far too simple to be effective, but for fishing a weed-covered bottom there can be no finer bait. The best flake comes from an uncut loaf, but don't get a crusty one. A 'sandwich loaf' is the one you want. Sliced bread is usable, but you don't get those big airy fluffy flakes that you do from an uncut loaf. Sliced bread is best used in conjunction with a bread punch. Lay the slice on the edge of your tackle box and push the bread punch down hard, giving it a twist. When you have some compacted flake in the punch, you insert your hook, pull out and then cast. Bread punch fishing is used when you're floatfishing and want a pinch of flake on a small hook size from 18 up to 14. Occasionally you can fish punched bread on a leger, but it is with floatfishing that it scores best.

Most of the time you will want to use a really large piece of flake on a hook size like a size 6 or 8. For this simply break off a piece of flake from the loaf about an inch square, flatten it once between your fingers, lay the hook in the middle then fold the sides of the flake around the hook, and pinch once. That's all you need. If you continue trying to mould it around the hook you can only make the bread into a dough ball which the hook has difficulty in getting through on the strike. When this flake sinks through the water it will expand and end up twice as large as when you squeezed it on. Make your first cast accurate, for the bread will undoubtedly come off once you move it. If you have any doubts, wind in, put another piece of flake on and re-cast. If you want to spice up the flake a bit, spray on some flavouring using an atomiser and one of the many flavourings available on the market. Flake is especially useful when fished over a weeded swim when you want a slow-sinking bait that rests on top of the weed where the tench can find it.

Following on from this basic tench bait you have worms, which are about as basic as you can get. For tench fishing I think you can put the worms into two categories—large and small! For lobworms, forget what you may have read in the old books about using only the tail of a lobworm. Even a 3-lb tench can slide a whole lobworm down its throat, so fish them whole, hooking through the body a couple of

Go Fishing for Tench

Profile of a tench. Tending to portliness, this big female tench gave a good account of herself on 4 lb line. All tench seem to give a good scrap and should be treated with respect, especially if near a snaggy swim.

times, using a size 6 or 4 hook. The smaller worms such as brandlings and redworms are best used in conjunction with a swimfeeder rig. Personally I like to use these smaller worms as a cocktail bait, tipping off say a bunch of maggots or a couple of grains of sweetcorn with a worm. I feel when small baits are getting a bit hard, then tench often mouth them but spit anything suspicious straight out. When they get the extra taste of that small worm it must switch them into a more confident mood as you get a good bite. Small worms are also effective when fished singly on a fine float tackle. With the best of the tench fishing being at dawn or dusk, I have found it possible to pick up the odd extra fish during bright daylight hours by fishing a small brandling on 2-lb line and a float in an otherwise 'dead' looking swim.

Possibly the best thing about worms is that they have a tremendous holding power when you chop them up and mix them in with the

Baits

Nigel Newport carefully slips back a tench that fell to a cocktail bait on fixed paternoster gear.

Go Fishing for Tench

Use a catapult when groundbaiting any distance out, as accuracy is all important if you use a swim marker. Where conditions permit, wade out and simply drop the groundbait balls into the swim.

groundbait. There definitely is something in a worm's body juices that drives the fish wild, so if you intend using them as a hookbait on their own, make sure you chop some up and mix them in with the feed.

There are times when you get a swim full of 'blowing' tench that just refuse every hookbait you put out. It was from a fishing friend, Adrian Hutchins that I first realised the significance of using groundbait paste. We were fishing Mytchett Farm Lake about twelve years ago, before anybody else even knew what was in it. Just another gravel pit they thought. I was after the pike, and Adrian was cracking out the crucians. Often he would get to 8 am with the sun well up and tench feeding avidly in the swim, yet have no bites on his hookbaits. He wondered if they were feeding on the tiny grains of groundbait. Mixing some of his groundbait into a paste he put some on the hook, cast out . . . and the rest is history as they say!

This is worth trying if you use heavily perfumed or scented groundbait additives as used by the continental matchmen. Sometimes the flavourings and herb concentrates in these groundbait additives are so rich that the fish ignore the hookbaits altogether and start feeding on the groundbait! So if you use a plain crumb groundbait, why not dip your hookbait into a bottle of flavouring before you cast. Only a small tip but one that might get you that extra fish or two.

Possibly one of the favourite tench baits is **sweetcorn.** The cheapest way to get this is by bulk buying from a cash and carry, you can get an even better price per weight if you buy it in 2-lb frozen bags (the only problem being that you can't bring it back with you if you don't use much, or find the conditions too bad to fish). With tins you can keep it as long as you want, although you should remember that a lot of clubs now ban the use of tins. Open them at the car when you have seen the conditions are fishable, and put the contents into a regular bait tin. The one drawback with sweetcorn is it goes off very quickly in hot weather, often before the end of a session, so throw in any leftovers rather than take the tin home. The smell of bad corn in a hot car really does give your nostrils a hammering!

With corn you have a very visual bait, but remember you also have the option of colouring them with one of the many colourings

Dave Barraball of Western Fuels Tackle shop took this huge haul of tench plus a few bonus bream after prebaiting with casters on a Hampshire Estate lake.

The author and Nigel Newport found trout pellet paste with strawberry flavouring the necessary killing bait for this tench bag of over 120 lb. The water is a noted carp water but the tench readily feed on baits used by the carp anglers.

Go Fishing for Tench

Mild spells in February or early March can produce surprising results for tench can suddenly come on the feed, even if only for short periods of time.

available at the tackle shops. This is especially helpful on a hard-fished water later in the season, when the tench start to get a bit wary of bright gold grains of corn. I always mix the juice from the tins into my groundbait, and many tench specialists using this hookbait liquidize a tin of corn for mashing into the groundbait mix. Corn can be fished as a single grain, or with several grains and tipped with a worm to make a bigger bait.

The most popular bait for tench, and most coarse fish has to be **maggots.** This hookbait must have accounted for more fish than all the other baits put together, but that's purely because it's the easiest bait to obtain and use. The best of the maggots for hookbait is the gozzer. This is a large maggot bred from liver, with some sugar to boost the size of it. Generally not widely available, the matchman has to get his own, but if you can buy some, do so. The ordinary white maggot, coming from the egg of the bluebottle is used both as a feed and a hookbait. A lot of anglers think maggots wriggle about all over the bottom. Drop some into clear water at your feet, then look there an hour later, when they are all drowned!

You can buy them in different colours, red, yellow, bronze, and at one stage a green-dyed maggot was available. I think colour has little bearing on a feeding tench, especially at night, but a red maggot does definitely have a slight advantage during daylight hours. This is borne out by a matchman's habit of tipping or using a hook with red maggots when the fishing gets a bit hard. The only logic behind this success may lie in the fact that the natural food of the tench, the bloodworm, is bright red. It's only a theory, but it might be worth trying red maggots.

Maggots are one of the only hookbaits that you can use as a live loose feed. Once you have put a carpet of groundbait down in your swim, I find it best to put in just a few maggots. Once the tench are established as being there, either by bubbling, line bites or a missed bite, then put in lots of loose feed. The maggot wriggling through the water, and obviously wriggling while a tench is in the vicinity, seems to excite them, and switches them from groundbait browsing to maggot eating in a very short space of time. If you put the maggots in with the initial feed too heavily, by the time the tench arrive in the swim, those maggots may be all dead on the bottom. Don't get me wrong, a tench is still going to eat them, but by waiting for the fish to establish themselves over the feed first, you can make them feed harder by the added attraction of a wriggling live maggot, rather than a dead one. Pinkies, as the smaller maggots are known can best be used as feed, with squatts, a small matchmen's standby feed maggot, being used for loose feed also.

One of the better small hook size baits to use is the **caster.** In fact I often think it's better than the maggot. The best caster colour is a light to medium brown. At this stage it will still sink, but leave it too long and it turns into a floater, useless for hookbait. Here's a tip you might want to follow up on. Many tackle shops turning their own maggots to casters have times when the weather is simply too hot to make this happen gradually, even with fridging. The casters turn to floaters and they throw them away. Try to get hold of these and squash them up in the groundbait mix, that keeps the fish in the swim longer, and the floaters will probably cost you nothing. Because turning maggots to casters at a regular rate is time consuming, you can be prepared to pay more for a pint of casters. However the best part of a caster is the fish popping that shell to get at the juices inside. The fly inside only hatches when the outer casing is a very dark brown, so if you get a load of floaters for nothing, you only need a pint of casters for hookbait and the occasional loose feed.

The carp angler's use of ready made **boilies** should also be tried by tench anglers, especially where the carp are fished for heavily with this bait. They can mop up anything they get inside their mouth, so it's a logical step to use some yourself. Some of the better flavourings for tench are very sweet, but with such a vast range of flavourings available, it may pay you to experiment. The carp anglers generally put out a carpet of the mini boilies, then fish a larger boilie as a hookbait over the top. In the case of the tench, just use the same mini boilies for hookbaits as you are using for the feed. Put out a carpet of groundbait first, then catapult out your loose feed of mini boilies over the top. Legering is the best technique to use, whether you put one, two or three boilies on the hook.

You can also make up your own **paste baits** for tench. The idea of boilies is to make a bait that can be left in the water for a long period of time without being nibbled away by the smaller fish. In contrast I

The tench, with one of the most effective baits yet to be fully exploited by the average angler. Mini boilies, as used by carp fishermen, are great baits for tench.

Match fishing brings in many tench during daylight hours when the traditional tench man has gone home. The reasons for success are fine tackle, small baits and a delicate approach.

Wading to reach the edge of a weedbed is worth the trouble. When summer weed growth extends far out into a lake, you may reach a clear area by wading out. This type of weeded water responds best to loose feed only.

At the start of each season, thousands of anglers start off by looking for tench. Late June offers every angler the best chance of a good catch – even breaking the 100 lb barrier. Once mid-July arrives, the fishing gets noticeably harder.

Use a disgorger or forceps to unhook these fine fish. Better still use barbless hooks.

A sight to warm the heart of most anglers. A fine net of fish taken by staying on into the first couple of hours of darkness. Dusk and dawn are the premier feeding periods for tench.

The author with a brace of Frensham tench weighing over 5 lb. These fish fell to link legered cocktail baits.

make my paste baits so soft I have trouble getting them to stay on the hook! Of course I recast every thirty minutes or so, just to check the baits. My base mix is made from trout feed. These are tiny floating or sinking pellets, which usually smell stronger the smaller in size they are. This is because trout fry require a higher protein intake than a larger fish, so the protein content is that much higher. You need to scald them with boiling water so they break down enough to mix, but at this stage you can put in added flavourings. After experimenting with several flavourings, I can honestly say there are two that do seem to boost my catch rate when standard pellet paste is failing: strawberry and freshwater mussel. The latter smells like nothing on earth, but is good for getting an initial bite on casting out, although it seems to die off through the sessions, while strawberry flavourings start a bit slower, but are more consistent with the number of bites they give you.

On top of these suggestions you have others like the real **freshwater mussel.** You use the mussel foot, the yellow part of the meat, the rest going for groundbait additive. **Hemp,** which is more of a feed than a hookbait. **Stewed wheat, sausage meat, luncheon meat** and of course **catfood** pastes. Almost anything will be eaten by tench at some time or other. What you as the angler have to find out is, a) the most productive bait for that water, or b) the bait most likely to secure the capture of a large individual specimen. The baits I have mentioned are my suggestions.

The Art of Prebaiting

Having established that the tench is primarily a bottom feeder, you must understand that to maximise your results you are going to have to put in a bit of extra work. Like so many things in life, you only get out what you are prepared to put in.

If you are approaching a venue strange to you, or a water that nobody is prepared to give you advance information on, then prebaiting is the best way for a good catch. Prebaiting basically means feeding a swim with your chosen hookbait or attractant, several days prior to your intended fishing trip. For many years, prebaiting was generally held as something to be done in the close season, to get fish interested that have been feeding on natural food. Now of course we know that prebaiting for tench can work, if not through the entire season, then certainly until the middle of August.

You may come across a water absolutely heaving with tench, but nobody has fished for them. By starting to fish straight away, you are going to take a few fish. But by taking time to assess the water, taking into account depth, fish movements, weedbeds, compass directions and prevailing winds, and couple this to a good prebaiting programme, I would say you could be all systems go for a massive catch.

It's not really important if the bankside vegetation is heavy or not. If it is, having predetermined your spot, you should set about clearing it just sufficiently to allow you to put out a chair, umbrella and bait cans. No need at all to hack down a ten yard area, even though it might seem like a good idea at the time. If there are nettles and brambles, set about cutting them with a sharp scythe on the end of a wooden pole. That way you don't get your hands torn or stung. If you need to trim back a few overhanging branches to allow for easy casting, use a handsaw if you can for neat cuts on branches, and a machete-style hatchet for trimming off the twigs. If your swim is in soft rushes, use those same branches to build up the swim to take your weight, and that of your tackle. If you use a keepnet, make sure there is enough depth of water at the side of the swim to cover all the rings.

Out in front of you, there may be all sorts of bottom or surface weeds. You do not need to drag the entire lake, as these same weedbeds provide both food and cover to the tench and other species. What you need to do is make a clear patch on the bottom so the feeding fish can find the bait, and thus ensure you catch them quicker. The type of weed and extent of growth will depend on the type of bottom you have on the lake bed. As mentioned previously, the tench love a soft muddy bottom, and it's here that you will get the dense weed growths. Some gravel pits are harder bottomed, still produce good tench, yet have less weed growth. Either way, there is no point in gambling on what the bottom is like. You want it clear and flat, with no snags, or masking weed fronds that hide the bait.

You need a basic understanding of water plants, so try to imagine

Baits

It is quite possible to gather together a variety of implements for dragging a swim properly. Here the author holds a curved scythe to which he can attach four extendable fibreglass poles, as used for tree pruning. Below him are three triangulated cutters made from mild steel bar and two commercial hacksaw blades. He then has a double blade cutter suitable for screwing in to a standard landing net pole. At the bottom is a large pair of commercial rakes, bolted back to back. To the left of the picture is a small double rake head with throwing pole. The latter is used · for dragging rather than cutting.

them as a garden underwater. These plants need the same substances for maintaining growth and regeneration as do their counterparts on the land. They need sustenance, in the shape of nitrates, carbonates, sulphates and phosphates. These materials are absorbed, not just through the root system as with land-based plants, but through the entire stem and leafwork. They tend to store the air in spaces between the stems, leaves and roots, as the dissolved oxygen content in water, especially a muddy lake, is never too high.

Probably the most readily identifiable of the surface leaves are the water lilies. These rarely grow in water of a depth of more than five feet, and are most prolific in the three-feet range, where they can smother a lake from end to end. If you fish a lake of regular mud bottom, the chances are that the wave action caused by the prevailing wind direction will have built up, or eroded silt at one end of the lake or the other. Most lakes usually have a shallow and deeper end, and the shallow end is where you want to start looking for the lilies. If there has been a natural growth here, the last thing you want to do is get in the middle and start ripping all the lilies out. The water depth will be the factor governing their growth, so where they stop growing can mean the water has a gradient into deeper water. What more could you want as an aid to fish location? You have two features in the shape of weeds for food and cover, plus a drop off into deeper water where fish will patrol.

You need to look for a natural break in this fringe of lilies, like a crescent shape with a few odd lilies in the centre. All you need to remove are those odd plants, plus a couple of channels into the lilies, directly opposite where you are casting to. This gives you a little extra space that allows you to overcast your baited area, and thus sink the line if you are floatfishing, or to straighten out the link, if you are legering. A small point, but one that a lot of anglers forget about. If you have to drag out lilies, use a rake head system to allow for the prongs to grip under the rhizome root system and tear them out completely. If you just snap off the stems and leaves, the knarled roots will provide a haven for hook links!

Water lilies are the traditional backdrop for tench fishermen, but these plants don't really hold a lot of the food chain. They are good cover for fish, but it's the bottom weeds that should interest the

Baits

Prebaiting a swim not only attracts tench, but gives you the added bonus of catching a variety of species. The author took this mixed bag of tench, bream and carp from a prebaited Hampshire lake.

77

angler most. Tench rooting about in the soft mud and weeds like water milfoil, hornwort and curly pondweed will send up clouds of bubbles. Dragging out a swim in this type of habitat is virtually guaranteed to give you a net of fish.

There are a couple of other weeds you should know about. Anglers know it as blanket-weed—long filamentous growths of fine fibres that cling to anything dragged through it. This is one of the thickest growths in shallow lakes with a lot of light penetration, and should be dragged out until clear. Spearblade, or arrowleaf lies flat on the surface like the lily. It grows in very shallow water, and as a general guide an area with this weed should be disregarded as being too shallow.

Canadian pondweed gives off a great deal of oxygen, and thrives in clear gravel pits with a silt bottom. There's plenty of food in it, and fish fry can find shelter to grow quickly without over predation.

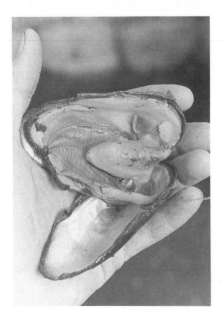

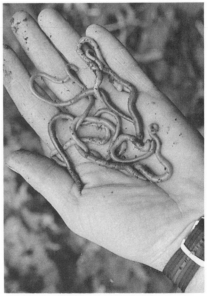

One of the few natural baits for tench. This swan mussel can provide up to two good baits for tench and is best fished on the bottom with a running leger rig.

Simple, yet highly effective. Worms and tench go together like cheese and wine. Worms are easy to get, so don't be afraid to fish them in bunches on a large size 2 carp hook.

However, too much of a good thing is not wise, and Canadian pondweed can completely choke a water. The tench love it, and can occasionally be seen drifting through on clear sunny days. This is ideal territory for the weed drag to be put into use, and I would be very disappointed not to get a good bag of fish from here. For raking a swim from the bank, you need to get equipped to do the job properly. To me, the preparation of a tench swim is like gardening underwater, with the exception that I don't have to plant anything! There are two ways of getting the weed out. You either use a weed drag that is attached to a long length of rope and which can be thrown out and pulled back or you can get in there with it using a pair of chest waders and do it with a long-handled rake. Depth plays an important part in the decision whether to use chest waders or not, so try to use a little common sense. Plumb the depth first and then wade out tentatively to see how soft the bottom is.

One of the easiest weed drags to make for bankside work is by tying two rake heads back to back, using just one handle. You can then wrap a length of chain around it after binding the heads together with wire as added weight. One of the basic rules to remember is tie the other end of the rope around something like your wrist or ankle. I must have lost three drags that sailed serenely out into the lake followed progressively by the end of the rope! This type of drag is ideal for Canadian pondweed, or anything else growing in the lake bed that is soft and fibrous.

For lilies and spearblade, you need to make a cutting drag. This is made in the shape of a triangle with two of the leading edges made from hacksaw blades. You can even use thin steel and grind a cutting edge on the blade with a file or grinder. Thrown out and dragged back, the blades should slice off any stems close to the bottom, but remember to follow it up with the rake drag that pulls out any remaining roots. Throw the drags out as far as you can because you need some clear ground behind where you intend baiting up for over casting. As previously mentioned, this is when floatfishing as you will need to wind the float back a few feet holding the rod tip under water to sink the line and prevent drifting.

Thirty or forty feet of rope should be sufficient to clear most swims, but for a better job you may need to get in there using either

If you have thick weed stems in the swim, or need to fish further out than the rake head can reach, use a throwing cutter.

Throw it well out, allow it to sink and strip back in hard short jerks to cut off any stems. Make sure you tie the other end of the rope around your wrist.

thigh boots or chest waders. The difference between these two types of wader is substantial, and if you can beg, borrow or buy a pair of chest waders, they will give you better comfort, especially in soft muddy lakes.

To do the job properly I advise first using the cutting drag by wading out and throwing it in a wide arc. It will obviously be farther than you need to cast, but it slows the regrowth of weed back to the swim. Then cover the ground again using a rake head drag. This removes most of the soft weed. Then, get a wide garden rake, and build it so lengths of sewer pipes or drain rods can be fitted to the head to make an extension. One I managed to borrow had screw-in extension poles made of hollow fibreglass. They came from those long tree snippers that can reach up twenty feet. Using this drag you can literally rake the bottom of the swim area you intend to bait, back and forth to dislodge any roots left or missed by the other two drags. In effect you are giving it a hell of a stir up! Do this part of the raking on a windy day, as the dislodged weeds will float to the surface and drift clear of the swim.

Let's say you reach this stage about five days before you want to fish. You will have to start thinking about putting some bait in, and the initial mix needs to be fairly substantial, but basic. Don't go wasting money on top groundbait or loose feed for this bait up. I make a bulk mix of bran, which only costs about £5 for a huge sack if you buy from an animal foodstuff wholesaler, and mix in anything I can lay my hands on; stale bread, cakes, biscuits and even some worms, still in the earth. Soak it well, and get out with the chest waders. Give the bottom of the swim a hell of a stir up, so clouds of mud and muck are mushrooming up to the surface. While this is all stirred up, dollop in this mix immediately. I do this because some of the groundbait will sink faster than the silt and mud particles in suspension, and will therefore be covered when it all settles. This makes the tench root about more to get the food, which in turn means they help to clear the bottom, and dislodge any loose shreds of weed. About two days after this initial bait up, you can drag again with the extending rake say two days or more later, but this time allow the silt to settle before baiting up with white or brown groundbait. Keep the groundbait mix of a coarse nature, only going

Using chest waders and a commercial size rake, get out as far as you can.

Use the full length of the pole and drag it back over the bottom.

Clean the weed off the drag, and either dump it on the bank or throw it to one side of the swim for the wind to clear.

When the weed is cleared, pump the rake head violently over the bottom to loosen all the gas bubbles held in the mud, and give the swim a thorough baiting up.

to fine cloudbait as the fishing gets harder.

A day or so before you intend to fish, mix in your required hookbait to the groundbait—maybe worms, sweetcorn or maggots. Make sure the hookbaits are thoroughly mixed, so the tench have to break open the groundbait to get the particles out. This makes them give more confident bites when you start to fish. The final bait up before the day you intend fishing need require no more dragging. Let everything settle down, and just bait up with crumb groundbait, letting it settle for fifteen minutes on the bottom. Then throw in your required hookbait, so that they rest on top of the groundbait. Simply fish the next day, but use only loose feed.

That should catch you a few tench, but should you fish a really soft-bottomed lake, you can hold the fish in the swim better, and make them bubble or blow, by mixing in blood and bone meal to that final prebait mix. You can use blood straight from the abattoir, but you need to wear rubber gloves for hygiene reasons. Also you will need to get hold of some anti-coagulant tablets from the chemists, and put these in the canisters of blood to prevent it clotting. This all sounds pretty disgusting, and I have no idea why blood holds the fish in the swim. It was used decades ago, and of course still works now. An easier way to do this is to buy dried blood in powder form from a wholesale garden centre. It seems to have risen in price quite a bit over the years, but at least you can use it when you want, and don't have to visit the abattoir! The only drawback is that today the dried blood has other additives, and while mineral elements must be all right in the water there might be some doubts with chemical additives.

Should you be fishing a larger lake you are going to need a boat to clear the swim. Follow the same procedure as with bank fishing, but if you remember, I made a point about clearing a couple of strips past where you have baited, to allow you freedom to overcast and wind back, thus sinking the line. You can set yourself up in a good boat swim, clear a patch in the lilies, anchor at dawn, cast out, and then the wind picks up! Sometimes even by sinking the line you are going to get some drag, so clear a circular swim, then make a clear strip at a quarter of the compass. That way, depending on the prevailing wind, or change in wind direction, you can alter the boat's anchored position to allow you to cast directly downwind. With the wind at your back, and provided you use good anchors, you can even tie your umbrella up.

The art of prebaiting lies not in the amount of feed you put in. Many anglers make the mistake of piling in tons of feed when there simply isn't the head of fish to eat their way through it. Then you get a build up of uneaten food that may sour the swim and prevent the fish moving in. The art lies in the preparation of the bottom. If you can get it completely clear of all snags and weeds, then the food can be located by the fish. Any hookbait you put in the swim should be visible to the fish, and not masked by fronds of weed. Also, apart from that initial 'heave-ho' with the bran mix, your groundbait prebaiting should be regular, rather than one great dollop. If it's at all possible to get to the water every day, do so. This is by far the best way to bring the fish on. If not, every couple of days will be OK, and anything over that means you really aren't getting the feed in regularly enough.

As well as taking into account what you think the head of tench may be, you should allow for the other species that will make inroads on that bait, roach, rudd, carp, bream and crucians will all move in on the easy feed. Probably they will be among the first to move in, but once a shoal of tench establish themselves over the bait, they will push all the other species out. Tench are nocturnal and dawn feeders. Therefore it will be best to put your prebait mix in early the previous evening. Then the tench will have the best chance of getting in on the feed first.

Now here's a problem you may come across now and again. If you have access to a little-fished water you may only see the odd angler now and then, but on a club water you will have 'swim-jumpers' to contend with. They will let you do all the ground work and prebaiting, then move in and fish the swim. I had an angler watch me rake and bait a swim on my local Fleet Great Pond, many years ago. He sat in the bushes with a camouflage jacket on and watched us through binoculars, obviously thinking we couldn't see him. As I had suffered swim jumpers on other club waters, I had no intention of finding his boat anchored over my mark, so what we did was to go out and taking bearings using a compass and eyesight, move the stick over to a useless stretch of water. He could see we had moved swims, but surely he would see us throw the bait in? Anticipating this, we mixed up the feed on shore, then positioned the boat and simply dropped the feed over the side that he couldn't see! Then we rowed over, dropped anchor at the stick, and pretended to mix up a bucket of feed—what was in fact filled with mud. We made a great show of throwing this out so he could see the splashes.

On open night I arrived with my boat to find him already out on the lake, anchored in position, right where our stick was. We simply rowed over, took our cross bearings with the compass and sight, anchored in our properly prebaited swim, and by the following dawn had a netful of prime tench and roach—while our swim jumper had precisely . . . NOTHING! To this day he doesn't know how we did it.

Of course, on the bank there will be a good chance that the person in the swim is quite genuine, and not an out-an-out swim jumper. He has paid the same funds and is perfectly entitled to fish there; it's just something you have to live with. I had it happen only last season at a club water near Yateley. I put in a lot of work, suffered a lot of wadersful of water, and introduced a lot of feed. The next day the angler hammered 20 tench from the swim, and was surprised how easy the fishing was! I certainly wasn't and never fished that swim again.

Some swim jumpers almost make an art out of scouting the water. Therefore if you drag your weed out don't dump it at the side of the swim. Take it down to the most awful looking stretch and lay it on the grass or reeds. To further draw them away, sprinkle a few hookbaits near the edge there, plus wet some groundbait and sink it on the bottom. That's a nice touch, and it's a real pleasure to see them setting up their stall with a mass of uncleared weed in the front of them.

Of course once you have a good hit from a swim, word soon gets round, and you can't get in there anyway. It's the price you pay, but I suppose it's natural for anglers to want to catch fish where it's easy. The trouble is few of them are prepared to put in the time and effort, not to mention feed, into the making of a tench swim. Now I clear two other backup swims, but don't bait them until the first starts getting fished too regularly.

Tackle

As with so many other sports, the subject of the best tools to use is often a personal choice. In fishing this is even more marked. The old saying that about ten per cent of the anglers catch ninety per cent of the fish is probably true, but it is often not the tackle itself that makes a successful fisherman.

The art of watercraft is the most important skill to learn for you can't catch fish that aren't there in front of you. Unfortunately it is not possible for me to put experience down on paper, and an in-depth knowledge of the species you wish to catch must be of paramount importance. Naturally there have been situations where a complete novice has walked up to a lake with inferior tackle, swung out a worm and caught the biggest fish in the lake. That's part of fishing, but while many feel this is luck, the pro anglers try to eliminate 'luck' as much as possible. Remember lady luck can be bad as well as good!

The top anglers can catch with inferior tackle. On one occasion out in the US state of Arizona I was on a press visit to Lake Powell. This was a massive body of water—189 miles long—created by damming the Colorado river. Although on a press trip to cover fishing, this day saw me with only a reel in the suitcase. Needless to say, on walking round the marina between the boats I found carp cruising . . . and with no rod available! After getting a loaf of bread from the marina store I arrived on the floating moorings with just a reel, four hooks and the bread. Hastily I found a five-foot piece of wood, tied some loops of line onto it for makeshift rings, and bound the reel on with more line. I threaded the line up it, tied on a hook, baited with a piece of bread, and after throwing some loose samples in, swung the bait out. It kissed the surface, absorbed water then sank slowly out of sight. I only waited thirty seconds before the line tweaked, I struck as hard as I dare and the water erupted. Carp number one was on! After a tussle it was unhooked and slipped back, possibly 4 lb in weight. Delighted at my attempts I ended up taking a total of five carp, pulled the hook on another three, then hit what looked to be a low double-figure fish, that hit the accelerator pedal, and ripped line from the reel so fast, the friction of nylon on nylon burned each ring through on my 'rod', and they twanged with each successive breakage. Finally the butt 'ring' burnt through and I ended up fighting the fish straight off the reel with this useless piece of wood stuck up in the air! Eventually, being unable to pump, the fish ran me under a pontoon, between two boats and cut me off on an anchor rope. So nobody tell me you need all the latest and greatest in expensive gadgetry to catch a few fish. It does make life easier, but isn't essential.

What you need is some good, high quality tackle that will do the job you require. If possible you want rods and reels that will double up for a variety of techniques, as that saves you more money. Looking at **rods,** I would have to say that if you can stretch to it, go for a carbon or carbon composite rod. While hollow glass is likely to stand a bit more maltreatment than carbon, the lightness and power of a carbon rod is still better.

Ryobi Masterline produce a couple of rods that will suit both float and leger work. The Avon/Quivertip is a specialist rod consisting of a butt and two top sections, one a standard Avon, the other with a spliced in quivertip. This means you can use the Avon top for straightforward legering with bobbin indicators. Fit the same top with a screw-in eye to take a swingtip, or simply change the tops when you want to quivertip. You can use a range of hook links down to 2 lb as the cushioning effect of the blank will prevent you breaking off. This carbon rod is fitted with sliding black anodised reel fittings, an abbreviated duplon handle, and has lined guides throughout. The top twenty-four inches of the quivertip section have been painted brilliant white for ease of bite detection. I would advise alternating red on the white for those surface glare swims mentioned previously. The rod is 11 feet long, rated for lines between 3 and 6 lb, and has a $1^1/4$-lb test curve, which is ideal for most tench fishing.

For floatfishing you can try the Ryobi Trident match series. They come in three different lengths: 10 feet, 11 feet, and 12 feet. I would opt for the 12-foot one. These are high quality black fibreglass blanks, with a sensitive tip for hook setting without risk of breaking off. They have ceramic lined tip and butt guides, with black hi-bell intermediate rings to prevent line stick in wet conditions. An abbreviated non-slip Duplon handle with sliding black anodised rings for reel attachment completes the picture.

As for choice of **reel**, the market is currently swamped with different makes and models. All will catch fish, but I will give you my opinion of which I think you should at least take a look at. The best reel for distance work and legering must surely be the Shimano Carbomatic. These reels have a unique dual drag system located at the rear which enables the angler to instantly increase or decrease the pre-set drag, yet just as easily return that same lever to the exact setting you had previously. It features a ceramic line roller, push-button graphite spools, three ball bearing races, a titanium graphite body and silent anti-reverse. This range of five reels has gear ratios ranging from 4:2 to 1 right up to 5:2 to 1. The GT1000X takes 165 yards of 4-lb test, the GT200X takes 180 yards of 6-lb test, and the GT3000X well over 350 yards of 6-lb test. If you really want a quality Shimano reel at the bottom of the range, take a look at the SGT-X-1000 which can also take 165 yards of 4-lb test, and is the cheapest in the range.

For floatfishing you may want to try a closed-faced reel. For that try the Ryobi Mastermatch. Weighing in at just 8 oz, the corrosion-resistant carbon body features an extra-wide graphite spool to prevent line bedding when retrieving under tension. This can happen when you have just fought a fish and the second cast is likely to fall short as the line drags off the bedded spool. This wider spool should help prevent that. It has a one-touch line-release knob, and backwinding is the method to play the fish. If you can't come to terms with a closed-face reel, and quite honestly they are easy to operate, try the Mastermatch MM300. This is a shallow-spooled open-face reel with a manually operated bail arm. It features a shortened reel stem which allows you to reach your index finger over easily to feather the rim of the spool during the cast; essential when you want to stop the float just prior to it hitting the water in order to avoid tangles. Its recovery rate boasts 33 inches of line with every turn of the handle, a silent anti-reverse, and it can be made ambidextrous.

For **lines**, I personally use only one for tench fishing, and that's Maxima in the 4 and 5-lb tests. It has a fine enough diameter to use as a straight-through terminal rig, and I simply like the way it disappears under water. It does have something of a memory for abrasion, so once you get it breaking, bin the lot and buy a fresh spool.

You'll need some **swimfeeders,** both the open ended variety for use with groundbait, and the blockend type with a fitted plastic cap at each end. If you are fishing near snags, buy some of the new swimfeeders that rise up quickly from the bottom on the retrieve. You may want to put an extension link of 10-lb line from the swimfeeder tiepoint to a small barrel swivel, in order that you can fish them as a link leger.

Of **floats** there are dozens to buy, and like me you'll probably end up with more than you ever use. Stick to bodied wagglers, all the same pattern, taking from a few bb up to three swan and they should cover you for most floatfishing eventualities. I see no reason to advise you on the old-fashioned crow quills etc, as modern floats are much more aerodynamic.

Now by law you have to use only lead-free or non-toxic **shots** and **weights.** If you buy bombs, make sure they are the pear-shaped Arseley bombs with a barrel swivel in the end. For bolt-rigging I would like to see a flat lead that suctions to the mud on the bottom. To the best of my knowledge there is nothing yet available on the market.

Hooks are another very personal item of tackle. The list of various patterns is almost endless, and I will recommend only two manufacturers, as even then you will have more choice than you will ever know what to do with. Mustad and Partridge hooks are the two makes to ask for, and as for sizes, well quite simply for big baits you need big hooks, and for small baits, small hooks. For maggot, caster, seeds and single grains of corn I would get some patterns in the sizes 18, 16, 14, and 12. For lobworms, bunches of maggots, several grains of corn, boilies and breadflake, get some 10s, 8s, 6s and 4s. They will take a big piece of flake on a size 2 carp hook, but you need go no larger than a size 4. Make sure the barb on the particular pattern you choose is not too high, not only because it makes it more difficult to extract from the fish, but because you'll find it penetrates easier on the strike. You may want to buy some spade end patterns for direct whipping onto the mainline, but I feel with such small eyes now available on many of the hooks, I think eyed patterns will suffice, right down to a size 18.

The main point to look for in a hook is that of fine wire and strength. You may have to try several patterns before you find one that suits you, but always ask local anglers for their favoured patterns. Although chances are they will all have a different choice, it helps eliminate your own time being wasted on patterns that might be totally unsuitable.

A few other items are worthy of mention when setting up for tench fishing. For **audible indicators** fished in conjunction with bobbins you will be hard pushed to beat the sensitivity of the Optonic. This small compact sounder registers both forward and drop-back bites, and is the mainstay of the specialist angler.

If you want to 'bag-up' on the tench make sure you have an adequate knotless keepnet. While tench are possibly the most hardy freshwater fish, there is no point in causing them any damage by cramping them in a small net. My own net has an 18-inch ring and extends to about 16 feet; more than enough space for the fish to lie comfortably. When you want to lift the net out for weighing and photographing the catch, make sure you lift the net from the bottom to the rim, while it still lies in the water. To do this properly you need to use waders, but at least you don't tumble them all down the mesh to crash on top of each other. Shorten them up until they are in the first two or three rings, then lift them . . . if you can.

Many anglers estimate the catch by how heavy it is. Try lifting just 60 lb of tench out, and they always shout out 'There's the ton . . . I knew there was 100 lb in there'. After this they photograph them, and proclaim the catch as being 100 lbs! I've caught a few bags over the magic 'ton' , and I always weigh the fish; no estimates, as I want to know the pounds and ounces of the catch. If you are one of those who constantly proclaims they have the 'ton', take the trouble to weigh them, and chances are you will be well short. Best way is to try and keep a mental note of how many fish you are catching, and add up the sizes. You need over 30 tench of more than 3 lb, and that's a lot of fish.

When photographing a bag of any species I always carry a large sheet of polythene. This prevents the fish getting damaged on rough gravel or covered in leaves. It also enables you to pick the whole catch up in the plastic by two of you taking a couple of corners each, and getting them in the water quickly. Don't ferry them back to the water one at a time. Tench are generally OK, but in hot weather they might get stressed if kept out too long. I make a point of weighing and recording the catch first, then putting them back in the net for a breather before lifting them out for a photograph. Another tip is to leave the keepnet over the top of the catch when you tip it out on the plastic sheeting. That calms them down a bit, although you may have to wait a minute or ninety seconds for them to stop flapping around. Remember they have regained their strength after being in the keepnet a few hours.

During the actual fishing session itself, keep either a plastic disgorger or a pair of forceps handy, as well as a torch if you are night fishing. Worms as bait are gulped down avidly by tench and you don't want to start fumbling round in the tackle box when the fish are in the swim and feeding. Put everything where you can find it.

Finally a word about the fish itself. Always be satisfied with catching a tench. At times they are easy, at times damned impossible. So never be too disappointed when it doesn't go as planned. As a photojournalist I've been out many nights high with expectation of 'doing the business'. Instead, the heavily prebaited swim rarely raises a bubble and I land just one or two fish. Having set out to catch a tench, just one fish of that species should justify the session. So make anything after that first fish a bonus, and you'll enjoy fishing for this powerful, yet secretive stillwater species even more.

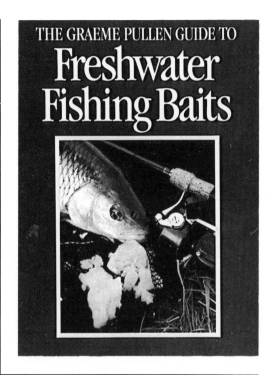

GO FISHING FOR

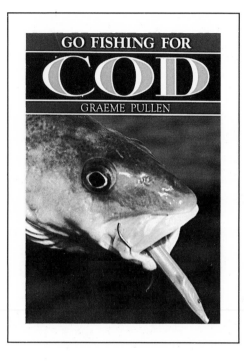

All available in the same series at £9.95 each.

96pp, 240 x 172mm
16pp colour and approx. 30 black & white photographs.